BLANCHE CONNELL

BOUNDARIES WITH TEENS

The Essential Guide on Understanding Your Teen, Discover the Ways on How You Can Help and Guide Your Teen Through the Teenage Years

Descrierea CIP a Bibliotecii Naționale a României
BLANCHE CONNELL
  BOUNDARIES WITH TEENS. The Essential Guide on Understanding Your Teen, Discover the Ways on How You Can Help and Guide Your Teen Through the Teenage Years / Blanche Connell – Bucharest: Editura My Ebook, 2021
  ISBN

BLANCHE CONNELL

BOUNDARIES WITH TEENS

**The Essential Guide on Understanding Your Teen,
Discover the Ways on How You Can Help and Guide
Your Teen Through the Teenage Years**

My Ebook Publishing House
Bucharest, 2021

TABLE OF CONTENTS

TABLE OF CONTENTS

CHAPTER 1

EMOTIONAL CHANGES FOUND IN ADOLESCENT GIRLS

Adolescence is a challenging time for all who pass through it. It is not easy changing from a child into an adult, and for girls there are many extra issues that can cause emotional upheaval. Here are some of those changes you may notice your daughter experiencing at this particular time in her life.

Moodiness

Moodiness is a normal part of adolescence, and your daughter may feel it dramatically due to premenstrual syndrome, more commonly known as PMS. Your daughter's monthly cycle can make her feel moody to the extreme, causing her to swing up and down emotionally.

You can help your daughter by encouraging her to participate in regular exercise, and eat foods that will stabilize PMS symptoms such as healthy fats from sources like nuts and avocados. Taking care of herself is something that will benefit both your daughter and those around her, and will be a skill that benefits her for her entire life.

Insecurity

Changes in friends, schools, body and emotions may cause your daughter to have many moments of insecurity. From feeling as though her friends have turned their backs on her, to times of not feeling totally comfortable with all the changes in her life, your teenage daughter is likely to experience many bouts of insecurity.

Remind her that no matter what changes may happen, you will always be her biggest cheerleader... and then be sure to back up your words with action.

Sensitive

Adolescence is the time in life where your words as a parent really count. Although this is always true, it is especially true knowing that whatever you say will make such a great impact - whether for good or not. This is a time in life when your child is feeling the most vulnerable to criticism. Choose your words carefully and think twice before correcting your daughter for trivial issues that can be overlooked.

Depression

Unfortunately, depression is becoming more and more common. If your daughter is walking through this, be the best support you can, and choose to love rather than judge. Encourage your daughter to talk to a counsellor or physician about her problem. There is help available if you know where to look.

Be aware for signs such as irritability, withdrawal from friends, and loss of pleasure in favourite activities that may signal a deeper problem of this nature.

Peer Dependence

It may drive you crazy, but peer dependence is one of the common emotional changes found in adolescent girls. While before you may have been your little girl's hero, you will now find her pulling away from you and drawing closer to her friends.

Instead of being overly critical of this, simply give your child the opportunity to find a good, solid group of friends. Involve your daughter in activities with those who may share her faith and personal interests, as this will allow her to branch out and find a variety of close friends that will last. Some of the friends that your daughter finds in her youth will be friends for life.

Adolescence is not easy for young women. With all the struggles faced by them, it takes much support and courage to make it through. Be the person your child can look up to and lean on in these challenging times of her life, and it will change her entire life for the better.

CHAPTER 2

EMOTIONAL CHANGES FOUND
IN ADOLESCENT BOYS

Your adolescent son may seem to be turning into a completely different individual than he once was. What is happening to him, and why? There are many changes, and reasons for them. Read on to discover more about teenage boys.

Anger

A troubling issue that many parents of teenage boys notice, is that their sons begin to display what seems to be a large amount of anger. There are a few factors that contribute to this, and it is a very normal emotion that comes into play at this part of a young man's life.

One part of the equation is the feeling that life is unfair, and the frustration and powerlessness that come with feeling more independent yet still having to deal with someone else making all the rules. You can partially avoid this issue by rewarding your son's maturity by giving him extra privileges and chances for independence.

Another part of the equation is the fact that puberty brings with it many hormones and chemical changes which influence your son's emotions. This can lead to surges of anger as he attempts to deal with these new feelings. As your son works through his anger, keep tabs on him to ensure that his anger is not an unending battle for him, as continuous anger can be a sign of depression.

Moodiness

Moodiness is another emotion found commonly in adolescent boys. The hormones that their body produces can lead to confusing feelings. This causes mood swings, and feelings that can fluctuate between excitement and fearlessness to feeling sad and low within a matter of moments.

Your son will often take his strongest feelings out on those he feels comfortable with, and since you are likely one of those closest to him, you will often bear the worst of it. This proves your son's comfort level with you, and therefore should not be always taken as a negative sign.

Isolation

Although teenage boys will go through periods where they want nothing but their friends, they may also display signs of isolation at times. This is normal as your son tries to figure out who and what he wants in his world. If your son is spending an extraordinary amount of time alone, however, it is important to talk to him and see exactly what is going on. Extreme isolation can be a sign of depression that needs to be dealt with.

Aggression

As puberty hits, aggression will rear its head in the lives of the boys who are going through it. This is necessary in part to help young boys become men who will stand up for important issues in life, and not back down.

Aggression can be used in a way that can benefit your son and others. It can also be channelled into physical activity that will help your son get in shape, and let him begin to feel good about himself. Enrol your son in a martial art of his choice, or any sport that requires determined participation.

Guiding your son through the emotional storms of adolescence does not have to be a constantly troubling situation. Instead, use the signs of emotional change that your son shows to learn more about him and where he is at. With your support, he will grow to be a stable and solid young man.

CHAPTER 3

WAYS TO INSTILL YOUR VALUES
IN YOUR TEEN

Although in most cases you are a parent to your child from the time your child is a newborn, the teens years are where your child's values are cemented into them and become a part of them that will continue into their future.

There is a lot you can do during the teenage years to encourage your child to hold fast to the values you have brought them up with to this point. Here are a few ideas to encourage this.

Continue to Build a Close Relationship between You and Your Child

One of the most important things you can do for your child is to maintain a close relationship with them through these crucial years. Be the listening ear your teenager needs, and be their friend as well as their parent. Spend quality time with them and consider them when making decisions.

Practice What You Preach

No child responds well to a hypocrite. If you are living one way and telling your child to live another, they will learn from your example rather than your words. If you tell your child to obey the law, but text while driving and consistently drive over the speed limit, your child will see through you and learn to disobey the law just as you do.

Don't Be Pushy

It is a difficult position to be in when you desperately want your child to inherit your values, while trying not to be pushy about it. When you force your thoughts and beliefs on children, they will most often rebel against them and walk away to choose their own path. Share your values with your teen, but let them choose their own direction.

Provide Structure

Your child may be growing up, but they still need basic care to help them do their best. Don't be heavy with rules, but do still have the important ones in place. Don't be afraid to say "no" when necessary, and be firm about your parenting decisions.

Carefully Choose the People Who Are Around Your Family

It is crucial that you use wisdom when deciding who will influence your child during both their younger childhood and their teen years. The people you allow around yourself and your child will become a strong voice in their lives. Give this position only to those whom you trust, and whose life principles you admire.

Be Calm

Although parenting during the teen years can be quite stressful, try to enjoy the ride. Don't get so involved in worrying about your child's future that you forget to enjoy the time you are spending with them now. Stay calm and be the most peaceful parent you can be.

Parenting teenagers can be stressful partly because you want your child to grow up to be a decent person who lives by strong values. Sometimes in the process, we can shift the focus from a relationship to pushing our beliefs onto them.

Be firm, disciplined, consistent and loving and you will see that your child picks up many of your values simply by seeing you live them. Enjoy these years and watch your child grow to become the wonderful, responsible adult you envision them to be.

CHAPTER 4

UNDERSTANDING THE INNER WORKINGS OF YOUR TEEN

Parenting a teen takes a combination of heart, skill, knowledge and intuition. One of your main goals as parent of a teen should be to understand their inner workings. This is essential in order to be able to help guide them successfully, and to get along in the process. Here are some things you will want to know in order to be the best parent you can be to your growing teen.

They Are More Emotional

Teens more often use the part of their brain that controls emotions than the part that controls logic and reason. Teens have also been shown to have a higher chance of misinterpreting facial expressions. This is a combination that can lead to great misunderstandings, and a resulting overflow of emotions.

Try to be gentle with your teen when it seems they are overreacting, as they may not be doing so intentionally.

They Are More Impulsive

Teens are known to be impulsive. In one way, this is a good thing because sometimes as adults we overthink situations without ever taking action. But being impulsive can also lead to unnecessary confrontations, and feeling let down by the results of the actions they thought would bring positive changes to their lives.

Be a sounding board for your teen when they need someone to talk to as they navigate these various disappointments.

They Are More Risky

Teens are prone to risk. Teenage boys are especially likely to engage in risky activities, but both genders engage in risk more than adults. With teens, the frontal lobe of the brain is not as connected to the rest of the brain as it is later in life. Because it takes longer to make a decision, your teen may come to a conclusion that a risk is worth it before being able to consider all the facts.

Risk is something that can make our world a better place, as many inventions are created and brave acts taken because of the courage of youth. Teach your teen the balance between risk and safety. Talk to them about natural consequences, and educate them fully on the possibilities of their actions. Encourage them to take their time making decisions, as this will prevent a lot of undue risks being judged as safe before they have the time to truly consider every aspect.

They Are More Sensitive

Have you ever disagreed with your teen and seen them dissolve into a pile of tears? You can blame their age. The high degree of emotion felt at this stage in combination with their largely social nature can combine to cause a high intensity of sensitivity. If they are not allowed to go to the party they wanted to, it does not simply feel disappointing, but life-altering.

Explain to your child that it is normal to feel this deeply sensitive and refrain from judging them over it, because otherwise they may think there is something wrong with them.

Your teen undergoes many changes as they grow and mature. Take every opportunity to validate your child's feelings and emotions, because this will help them understand that the teen years are a time of much change, and that it is ok to feel and act the way they do. With a strong sense of support, your teen's adolescence can be a mainly positive experience, and lay a firm foundation for the rest of their life.

CHAPTER 5

TIPS TO HELP YOUR TEENAGER GET THE MOST OUT OF SCHOOL

Attending school is one of the most important things your teenager will do with their time. Junior high and high school will fill up a large part of your teenager's life, and there are many things you can do to help this part of their life run smoothly.

As your child gets older, your part in their life will become less about giving commands and more about giving support. Here are some ideas on how you can help your teenager get the most out of school.

Encourage Learning to Speed Read

This is a tangible skill that will help your teenager study more quickly. The amount of reading material they will be assigned in this phase of life is significantly more than when they were in their younger years. There are many different ways to speed read, so encourage your child to try a few and decide on the method that works best for them.

Encourage Learning to Focus

When your child was younger, they may have been able to get away with not fully focusing on the material at hand. Learning to focus is important as they enter their teen years.

Help your child to figure out how to remove distractions when they are experiencing difficulty focusing. Teach them to remove possible distractions one by one, such as turning off music, powering down their smartphone, or closing any windows that open onto a loud, busy street.

Encourage Regular Study Time

Your teenager will need to learn to study regularly if they do not want to become stressed because of leaving everything until last minute. It is far more beneficial if they build the skill of setting aside a certain amount of time each day to study. This might be 20 minutes per day, or it might be three hours per day. What is important is not so much the amount of time, but your child's consistency.

Encourage Inspiring Friendships

The individuals your child chooses to spend time with will change their course of direction over time. If your child chooses friends who inspire them to build their character and who encourage them to work hard in life, your child will generally walk down the same path. If your child has more friends who are interested only in having fun, your child's grades will likely suffer, as could their future.

Encourage Good Nutrition

Nutrition plays an important role in giving the brain its power. Although junk food is a common part of the life of most teens, teach your child to keep the main amount of their food intake healthy. Fruits, vegetables, lean proteins, whole grain carbs and healthy fats should be your child's main source of nutrition. Consider supplements if your child is a picky eater, or if their diet is lacking in any way.

Encourage Routine

Although your teenager's routine is sure to be different than when they were little, it is still an essential part of keeping things running smoothly. Talk to your child about regular meals, regular bedtimes and getting enough sleep each night. This will give their body a chance to know what to expect on a daily basis, and their body will then provide them with better results.

You will be your teenager's greatest source of help as they go through these challenging years. Take every opportunity to share your wisdom with them in regards to how to live it well. With your efforts, your teenager will be sure to glean a lot from their school years.

CHAPTER 6

HELPING YOUR TEEN DEAL WITH CONFLICT IN A POSITIVE MANNER

Conflict is difficult to deal with, and it is especially tough in the adolescent years. Your child is already going through many changes in their body and mind. Conflict simply adds another complex layer to a time in life where things may already feel as though they are in an upheaval.

By supporting your child through any conflict they find themselves in, you can be a stabilizing voice in their life. Here is how you can help your teen deal with conflict in a way that will help them to push through the tough times and find their way to a better place in life.

Learning from Mistakes

Always remind your teen that although conflict is laborious, it is a sure way to learn different kinds of lessons. We can all learn from our mistakes. This means we can explore and find a tangible lesson, and then go forward while being able to avoid the same pitfalls in the future.

Using Conflict to Learn about Themselves

When there has been a disagreement, it is a rare opportunity to search inward and learn about oneself. There are many lessons you can find if you are determined to learn them, and this is important for teens to realize.

Maybe your teen will come to the awareness that he (or she) does not fight in a fair manner, or that he holds his feelings in until he bursts in a dramatic way. Or maybe he will find something positive, such as his strength when forced to stand alone on an issue.

Using Conflict to Learn about Others

Conflict is a great way to learn about others. Your teen can learn about what kinds of friends, family and other individuals are in their lives based on how conflicts arise and play out. Teach your teen to decipher whether the other party is still supportive during conflict, or whether they are using it as an opportunity to push your teen down. Is the other party fair and honest, or angry and deceitful? Conflict will reveal all.

Using Conflict as a Springboard to New Opportunities

It is said that unless we grow uncomfortable where we are, we never have the motive necessary to make changes. Conflict can sometimes cause your teen to want to move beyond where they are at the moment.

Maybe being in constant conflict with their boss will push them out of their current workplace and into the job of their dreams. Perhaps conflict experienced with a current boyfriend will prove to your daughter that she deserves better in a partner, and will prompt her to break up and move on.

Be an Emotional Support

During times of conflict, your teen will need your unconditional love and support. Be a strong role model and teacher of how to deal with negative encounters, and most of all let your teen know you will always be there for them.

Spend quality time with your teen and help them get their mind off of their problems. Know when to discuss, and when to suggest taking a mental health break and heading to the mall to grab an ice cream together.

Conflict will be difficult for your child, because conflict is difficult for everyone. You will be one of the main guiding supports for your child as they navigate it. Use this opportunity to teach your child about growth, friendship and self-care, and they will keep those lessons for life.

CHAPTER 7

HELPING YOUR TEEN EFFECTIVELY DEAL WITH BULLYING

Bullying is something that is unfortunately happening far too often in our society. Gone are the days where there were a few bullies per school who picked on kids but were kept in place by teachers and societal norms.

The innovation of modern technology, although it has benefits, has brought along with it some very negative circumstances - one of them being widespread bullying. Here is how you as a parent can help your teen deal with this difficult situation.

Why Do People Bully?

Bullying happens when someone directs their hurt, anger and frustration at another individual. Perhaps the bully feels invisible, and is being ignored or hurt by important people in their lives.

Low self-esteem, difficult home situations, jealousy and intolerant ways of thinking can cause an individual to use bullying as their way to relieve their anger or make themselves feel more important by belittling others. There are many reasons for bullying as there are bullies.

Why Does Bullying Seem to Be So Common?

Bullying has always been around, but with the creation and popularity of the internet and social media, it has grown out of hand. Instead of teens being able to escape bullying when they leave school or extracurricular activities, their issues follow them everywhere. Online stalking is becoming more common, where bullies will follow and harass their victims and refuse to leave them alone at any time.

Another reason for the amped-up bullying that is taking place can be attributed to more interactions among people, which can lead to attacks on people for what they believe by small-minded individuals.

What Bullying Does to a Child

Being bullied lowers a child's self-esteem. It causes them to feel insecure, and is a catalyst for depression and anger. Bullying can eventually lead to the victim becoming a bully, in an attempt to take back the power from those who hurt them.

Teens who are bullied begin to find it difficult to trust anyone, and this feeling often lasts into adulthood.

How to Help Your Bullied Child

Teach your child about their rights as an individual. If your child is being discriminated against and made to feel unsafe, the law is on their side. Hate crimes are illegal. Every teen has the right to feel safe and secure, and free from the threat of violence.

If your teen is being bullied, contact the appropriate authorities, whether that is the authorities at school or the police. Train your child in the proper way to deal with bullies, and role play different scenarios to assist your child in finding their voice and means of fighting back.

Monitor your child's internet use, and ensure that he (or she) is not being threatened or intimidated by others. Above all, teach your teen to trust his intuition. If he is responding to bulling in a proper way, but begins to realize that it is not working, let him know that it is ok to change his course of action partway through an interaction.

If your teen is being bullied, you are his greatest advocate. Use your voice to stand up for your child, and be his safe place to land when he needs someone to talk to. Let your teen know that he is important and worth protecting.

CHAPTER 8

TEENAGE GIRLS AND SOCIAL MEDIA

Like it or not, social media is one of the most popular methods of communication in the era that we live in. No matter what your daughter is doing on social media, it is almost guaranteed that she is on there in some form. It is important for you as a parent to know what is happening on social media so that you can be aware of the benefits and downfalls of it, and can protect your child from the possible dangers.

How Social Media Influences Teenage Girls

Social media is the new way to stay in touch with all that is popular. Whether it is searching for new hairstyles, forwarding memes, or participating in group chats, social media is taking up a lot of time in the lives of adolescent children.

Social media can be used for good, helping your daughter to stay in touch with her friends and distant family members. It can also be used for negative things, such as exposing your daughter to the unpleasant thoughts of others, as well as allowing tragic situations such as online bullying.

What Teenage Girls Are Doing on Social Media

Your daughter is doing many things on social media. It is more than likely she is connecting with friends. With sites such as Facebook, Twitter and Instagram, it is easy to connect with others so that individuals can share photos, jokes and fitness videos among many other things. Your daughter is probably building networking skills as she meets friends of friends and connects with them on a slightly personal level.

Sending and posting photos is also, of course, a very popular thing to do on social media. There are personal photos shared, humorous photos and pictures of the latest concerts and events your daughter has participated in.

Another thing your daughter is able to do on social media is to research her interests. From fashion to pop culture to music, your teen can find it all online. Her and her friends will likely post, share, and send links to each other about whatever is popular at the moment. The internet and social media in particular is amazing in the opportunities it provides for research in any area one is interested in.

How to Prepare Your Daughter to Use Social Media Responsibly

Social media is a great opportunity, but it can also be dangerous. There are several steps your daughter should take before she joins any social media sites, or views anyone else's.

First, talk with your daughter about where she is at. Is she able to participate in public, online conversations without getting too involved? Does she know the dangers of keeping important and personal information private? Is she dedicated to

29

not only avoid bullying situations, but also to stand against them? Is she willing to put time limits on herself, and show responsibility in her use of social media?

Take steps to assist her in becoming accountable in her use of social media. Some suggestions include adding her as a friend or contact on whatever particular medium she is involved in, and letting her know that you will be regularly checking in on her by using a password that is known to both of you.

For teens, social media is going to be around a long time. Although certain social media websites may come and go, this way of keeping in touch will be around awhile. Use this opportunity to help your daughter navigate a new experience which will assist her life skills long term.

CHAPTER 9

Teenage Boys and Social Media

Social media has a huge impact on young people today, including young men. Teenage boys are on social media a great deal, even if they tend to do different things than girls do when they are on it. If you are interested in what your teenage boy is doing on social media and how you can help him use it wisely, then keep reading.

How Social Media Influences Teenage Boys

Social media has an influence on most children who use it. Teenage boys are drawn into the fun aspect, and find it easy to bond with others friends who are online, along with the fact that they can easily turn it off when they get bored.

Its influence is shown in how often teenage boys are online, and how much they talk about it when they are not. If you spend any time at all with adolescent boys, you will hear how much they quote and think about what they see online on various social media outlets. Not only do teenage boys enjoy spending time surfing on social media, it also has an influence on their social perspective and opinions.

What Teenage Boys Are Doing on Social Media

Although male teens spend a lot of time on social media, as do their female counterparts, they tend to use it differently.

Some of the things you will notice your teenage son using social media for is sending jokes and memes to his friends, and researching interests such as vehicles, sports and sports figures. He will use social media as a way to find more articles on those interests, and will post about these topics himself.

A huge component of social media for boys includes online gaming. In fact, this is one of the biggest social media type outlets that you may notice your son spending time on. Online gaming attracts boys because of its competitive nature, and provides a way for him to connect with his friends through this means. Many young men even meet online friends this way, playing games regularly with the same group of people they come to know as an online presence.

Of course, social media would not be complete without the added attraction of an easy way for boys to meet girls and converse with them, especially during the earlier teen years which can be awkward for both genders.

How to Prepare Your Son to Use Social Media Responsibly

It is very important in this age of easy internet access that you teach your teenage son to act responsibly when online and when using any social media outlet. Without social media etiquette and a sense of personal responsibility, the online world can become a dangerous place.

Give your son rules such as a time limit on his internet and social media use, and conduct careful parental monitoring in regards to whom he is contacting online. Educate him on his personal responsibility not to join in online bullying, and make it clear to him that he can come to you if he is feeling threatened by anyone in any way.

Social media is a huge part of the life of modern teenage boys, and will likely continue to be for quite some time. By learning more about your son's social media use, you will become a better parent. Steer your son in the right direction, as he participates in what is now a cultural norm and will continue to be for years to come.

CHAPTER 10

WHAT TO DO IF YOUR TEENAGER BREAKS THE LAW

It can be overwhelming and discouraging when your teenager breaks the law. There are mixed feelings of wanting to protect your child yet wanting them to taste the consequences. Here are some ideas to help you navigate through this difficult time as a parent.

Be Supportive

We all make mistakes and bad choices. Teens have challenges related to their growth and hormones that make them even more likely to be a poor judge of situations, which can lead to bad decisions. No matter what caused your child to break the law, or what law they broke, be supportive of them as an individual and as your child. You can support your teen without condoning their actions.

Hold Them Accountable and Think about Long-Term Consequences

Don't be the kind of parent who lets their children slip through the cracks, the type of parent who causes trouble without learning through consequences. Hold your child accountable and let them know that it is because you love them that you will insist that justice be served, even if it is a tough situation for them.

You are not doing your child, yourself or society any favours by trying to rescue your child for their consequences. If your child finds that you will bail them out of any situation they put themselves in, they will begin to expect that and become trapped in more and more trouble. This will create a teen who becomes a self-entitled adult who never learns, and who becomes a drain on society.

If your child has committed a crime and you know about it, report him (or her). Don't turn a blind eye simply because it is your child participating in the wrong behavior. Know that your tough love will help create a responsible citizen who takes ownership and responsibility for their actions and decisions.

Don't Blame Yourself

Although our parenting certainly plays a role in how our children turn out, they are also individuals who make decisions and life choices on their own eventually. When your teen is living on the edge and is making many wrong choices and surrounding themselves with bad influences, there is often nothing you can do. You can certainly give your child consequences, but there is nothing you can do to change who they are on the inside. Give yourself a break and continue to love yourself.

Continue to Show Love

You can love a child who is doing wrong, even if you strongly disagree with the choices they have made. Loving your son or daughter even as they break the law does not mean you condone their wrong behavior. This love you give them is actually necessary for your child in order for them to feel it, know it and to assist with bringing themselves out of their self-destructive behavior.

Parenting a teen is not easy, and it throws an extra complication into the mix when your teen breaks the law. Be firm with your child, but continue to love him thorough the mess he has created. In time, this support will bring your child hopes of a better future.

Printed by Libri Plureos GmbH in Hamburg, Germany